AF488410

ABCs

with LISI
The Search and Rescue Dog

By Preston & Kayle Burns

Illustrated by KidsBook Art

Meet Lisi the Golden and the Burns Family!

Photo: Katie Young, Keystone Resort

Hi, I am Lisi the Golden Retriever! I am a real life Search and Rescue dog living in the Colorado Rocky Mountains. My best friend and handler, Preston, works with me at the ski resort.

You may think my name is a little silly, but that's because my florist mom, Kayle, named me after her favorite flower, Lisianthus. You can pronounce my name as liss-e.

This book is dedicated to my little sister, Delaney. ~ Lisi

Photo: Katie Young, Keystone Resort

Follow Me in Real Life!

 @lisithegolden

Illustrated By:  @kidsartbook23

An **Avalanche** is when snow quickly falls down
a mountain slope. My handler and I are trained to search
avalanche terrain in an emergency situation.

On snow days, I get to wear **Boots**.
Boots help keep my feet warm and help
protect my feet from getting ice and
snow stuck between my toes.

Chairlifts are used to move skiers and snowboarders to the top of the mountain. I love riding chairlifts too!

Since I can't talk, I **Dig** to communicate with my handler.
If I start digging in the snow, that tells my handler I found something!

I may be a dog, but I wear protective **Eyewear** when I am working. My goggles help protect my eyes from the snow, wind, and the intense sun.

I love going to work because I have the most **Fun** with my handler. He challenges me with new games and I even get to ride a snowmobile!

Another way to get to the top of the mountain is on a **Gondola**. A Gondola is an enclosed cabin that keeps you nice and warm. I love riding the gondola because I get to look out all the windows!

My favorite way to get from peak to peak is in a **Helicopter.**
The view from the helicopter makes the world below seem so small.

When I make a find, I **Indicate** to my handler by digging.

When my handler and I need to get around the ski resort, I **Jump** on his shoulders and enjoy the ride as he skis down the mountain.

I work for a resort in beautiful **Keystone**, Colorado.
It snows more than 60 days a year, totaling almost 200 inches.

I couldn't do this job without my **Loyal** handler.
We love and support each other in everything we do.
Do you have a loyal friend or dog too?

I love living in the **Mountains**. My best dog friend, **Māia** (MA-Ya), is also a Search and Rescue dog. We have the most fun playing in the mountains!

My **Nose** is my superpower! Did you know a dog's sense of smell is
10,000 to 100,000 times more powerful than a human's?
That's why my nose is my favorite tool to use when searching.

Being a working dog takes a lot of **Obedience** training.
My handler teaches me special commands and
when I obey, I get rewarded.

Our favorite days are **Powder** days!
The snow is so soft and fluffy and we have tons of fun.

A **Quarry** is the person that hides from me in training. I am really good at finding people even when they have the best hiding spots. Do you like to play hide-and-seek too?

I have lots of jobs, but my most important job is to help
Rescue people from dangerous situations.

My handler is a **Ski Patroller**. He and his friends are responsible for keeping skiers and snowboarders safe on the mountain. They will help you if you are hurt or you are lost. They are easy to spot because they wear red jackets with a white cross.

Tug is my favorite game to play with my handler. We get to play tug when I successfully find what I am searching for. It's the best reward!

Remember my superpower nose?
It even helps me smell things **Under** the snow!

When I am working, I wear a special **Vest**. When you see a dog wearing a vest that usually means it is a working dog too. Always ask before petting working dogs because you may be distracting them from their job.

I am just one type of **Working Dog**. Other dogs have jobs too! Some work for the police department, some provide comfort when people are sad, and some even guide people that cannot see.

If you ever go skiing or snowboarding, you may see my dog friends
and I working on the mountain. We may be **eXtra** cute,
but remember, you have to ask to pet us first.

When I do a good job, my handler gives me **Yummy** treats.
My handler always has treats close by so he can reward me.

I am the sleepiest dog after work. I always look forward to dinner and catching some **ZZZZs** at the end of my busy day. Just like you. Night, night!

9 798218 358761